T0381028

The Wilber Effect

Effect

Seeing Beyond Limitations in Life and Career

by Cindi N. Koch

Balboa Press books may be ordered through booksellers or by contacting:

Balboa Press
A Division of Hay House
1663 Liberty Drive
Bloomington, IN 47403
www.balboapress.com
1 (877) 407-4847

ISBN: 978-1-9822-1672-6 (sc)
ISBN: 978-1-9822-1673-3 (e)

Library of Congress Control Number: 2019903319

Print information available on the last page.

Balboa Press rev. date: 03/29/2019

BALBOA.
PRESS
A DIVISION OF HAY HOUSE

The Wilber Effect

Cindi N. Koch

To everyone who has ever felt stuck, with no idea why. This one is for you!

Bart—thank you for your unconditional love through all the choices and changes we have made together for a lifetime. Your support is my encouragement, especially in helping me bring life to this story.

My precious family—thank you for your love and support every day and always!

Danita—I am grateful for your wisdom, patience, and being part of life's journey. Most of all, thank you for being my Tilley!

Theresa—thank you for your enthusiasm and wit and mainly for lassoing a butterfly and encouraging her to sit in her chair!

Pink Gator Press—thank you, Chanelle, for bringing Wilber to life!

PREFACE

Our lives can change by choice or by necessity. The one thing life guarantees is change. Given that change is inevitable, you do not need to be as frightened of it as many seem to be, especially when you know how to make appropriate choices to manage change.

What motivates you? Conversely, what stops you from moving forward? When we were children, we had no problem dreaming big dreams, but as grown-ups, we have learned to be more constrained. We can clearly identify what we do *not* want; however, we struggle when we try to identify what we aspire to. This struggle creates a disconnect between what we dream of and what we actually drive toward. Until we align our desires with our actions, the things we want will never materialize.

You make choices everyday with your thoughts and words. Realizing your role in the creation of your path is one of the most important lessons to learn. Wilber starts out wanting more in his life, meets a mentor who shows him how to create a new life in a new way, and then takes action on what he learns. Because of his changes, his friends and family begin to see a bigger picture and understand self-responsibility as a way to success. The situations Wilber goes through can be taken as deeply as the reader wants to go.

So many people experience roadblocks on the way to accomplishing their dreams, never realizing their own role in creating these roadblocks. When limitations surface, and it feels like you are possibly headed toward hot water, and you decide it is time to become "unhampered," take a deep breath and begin answering the questions that will set you on your way to creating more of what you want in your work and life—however you define it.

As you read *The Wilber Effect*, you will find it applies to situations and experiences in everyday life. When you live hampered, you give up on hopes and dreams. In contrast, I have seen people become more deliberate cocreators of their lives simply by putting themselves into the creation. My hope for you is that *The Wilber Effect* will help you unhamper your dreams. I encourage you to read it a second time and substitute your name in place of Wilber's for a more personalized interpretation. As you create your adventures, stay curious, and carry the confidence to create the unhampered life you want.

Whether you are facing, chasing, or embracing change, the basic strategy is the same: it all starts with *you*!

It is my belief that

what we think about, we talk about;

what we talk about, we believe; and

what we believe, we create.

Once you grasp the connection between the above statements, you have taken the first step toward creating the life you want. The fable of Wilber might sound simplistic, and that is by design. I want you to be as comfortable with the idea of change as you are with taking your next breath!

Chapter 1
CHANGE HAPPENS!

Wilber was a blue crab who lived in a bayou in southern Louisiana. (For those who are unfamiliar, a bayou is where the salt water from the Gulf of Mexico meets the fresh water from inland streams.) Wilber's bayou had shrimp boats, cypress trees draped with Spanish moss, and an abundance of

wildlife. Adding to its splendor were creatures like alligators, catfish, crawfish, and, of course, crabs. It was a fun place to live!

Wilber was a happy crab. He and his family and friends, collectively known as a cast of crabs, lived in a community. They worked together and helped one another collect food and protect their families. They treated one another with respect and love, most of the time. They had fun together every day. Since his home was close to a wooden dock on the bayou, Wilber saw the shrimp boats, with their nets, not too far away. Wilber had been taught about the dangers of boats and nets. It was best to stay far away!

The crabs were comfortable with the home they had created on the bayou floor. They had no desire to leave and explore new areas. Wilber, being a savvy crab, acknowledged that his cast were happy to stay together in what they considered a safe environment. He knew he could stay there as long as he wanted. In fact, most of the cast would have preferred he stay close to the group, but that was not really what Wilber wanted. Even though Wilber loved and enjoyed his home, he wanted more. He wanted to explore. The first time Wilber knew he wanted to explore was the day he crawled up on a log on the far side of the bayou. He saw higher and farther than ever. He looked around in every direction. It was amazing!

He took in all the colors and interesting sights he hoped to explore one day. Wilber wasn't sure whether leaving would be safe or whether he would like it. He just knew he had to find out what it would be like. He dreamed of venturing out, seeing new things, meeting other crabs, and returning to his cast with tales from afar.

"What is this coming at me?" Wilber asked.

As the critters flew closer, Wilber saw they were beautiful yellow butterflies. They flew so close that Wilber knew they were saying hello. The beautiful butterflies made Wilber feel happy. From that day forward, butterflies held a positive and special meaning for him.

He never shared his ambitions with his cast. In situations like this, when others were satisfied where they were, Wilber knew it could be disruptive to share his desires and beliefs about what he truly wanted. He had watched the crabs roll their eyes and shake their heads when a new idea was discussed. Wilber felt the disappointment from the cast, and he allowed fear to stop him from sharing. It was easier to go along and get along with the others.

Today, though, he was feeling more tenacious and strong-minded about leaving his safe environment to explore. Wilber had, in fact, decided it was now or never. He took a deep breath and made the decision to tell the other crabs his plans.

Personal Perspective

Is Wilber's cast of characters similar to those in your life? Have you ever captured, in writing, all the things you have always wanted to do?

Chapter 2
CHANGE: OPPORTUNITY OR ROADBLOCK?

Just as Wilber was ready to make his big announcement, the unthinkable happened. He and his cast found themselves tangled up in a fisherman's net. After swinging in the air and being bounced up and down, the crabs realized what had happened. They had been swept up in the net while the fishermen were cleaning out their boat. The next thing they knew, they were tossed inside a hamper.

In a flash, everything had changed!

While the others were busy working, a fisherman placed the hamper (a wooden basket used on the bayou to temporarily hold crabs) on the dock. Crabs were not what they were fishing for, so they had no use for the crabs. The men intended to throw them back into the bayou, but the crabs didn't know that.

Confused by the sudden change in their environment, the crabs immediately moved sideways, which is what crabs do, especially when surveying new surroundings. They had seen a hamper before but not from the inside! Not only were they in a new space, but they were faced with new challenges.

Only Wilber saw opportunities. He overheard the fishermen talking. They weren't worried that the crabs would crawl out. They understood the nature of crabs. If you place one in a hamper, it will crawl right out. Interestingly, if you place a bunch in a hamper, they all sit together. They are able to crawl out but usually don't. And if one does try, the others immediately pull it back. The fishermen—and Wilber—were confident that the cast would stay in the hamper.

Wilber overheard the other crabs telling stories to one another about the danger of leaving the group, especially now that they were stuck in a hamper. They quickly discovered they could see their bayou! It felt very far away. Although they knew they had been taken out of their comfortable home, the main chatter was about gratitude for their safety and for being together. Wilber agreed. He went along with the group until his mind grew restless, and he wondered what options were available to his cast.

Wilber said to the others, "Even though I enjoyed living in the bayou, I thought it was too small—but this hamper is never going to be good!"

Other crabs said, "Oh, Wilber, please don't talk about leaving the cast and exploring. We know exactly where we are. Just wait—something will happen. We're safe for now."

"Are you still in shock?" Wilber blurted. "We have to plan how to get out of here!"

Some of the cast could see Wilber's point, some were mildly irritated, and some continued to ignore him. Regardless, the other crabs wanted no part of Wilber's crazy ideas for leaving the hamper and returning to the bayou. They couldn't imagine how they could achieve something so monstrously big and dangerous. They collectively decided their best choice was to settle in and wait to see what happened.

But Wilber couldn't stop thinking of escape. *Exploring has always been what I wanted to do. Now that I am out of the bayou and on top of the dock, I will not have so far to travel!* Wilber saw how exploring from the top of the dock could be exciting and possible.

Remembering what the fisherman had said earlier, Wilber thought, *Maybe I could be the one crab who crawls out.* His mind soared with excitement.

Wilber faced a big decision: Settle in or move on?

Personal Perspective

Are you comfortable with following your dreams regardless of what others think?

Chapter 3
LEADERSHIP, COURAGE, AND ACTION

After thinking over his options, Wilber declared, "I *am* going to be the one crab who crawls out of this hamper!" It was time to tell the other crabs that he was planning to leave the hamper and explore. Predictably, it did not go well.

When word got around regarding Wilber's dream and action plan, it became obvious that many of the crabs were disturbed. "What's wrong with him?" was the constant question asked by the cast. "Doesn't he know that it is unsafe out there? We have everything we need right here. Why would he want to leave?" "Will his recklessness bring additional danger our way?"

The more Wilber talked about what he wanted to see and do, the more the cast resisted. Their negative comments and his indecision hurt his crab brain! Wilber instinctively knew the time had come to decide whether he would listen to the other crabs or make his own decision and chart his own path. He realized it was easy to be an independent thinker when he was alone. However, when he was surrounded by those who did not welcome change, it was much more difficult for him to stay focused on leaving.

Wilber moved away from the others to ponder what had happened since he'd announced his ambitions. He had known he would get some resistance, but this was almost more than he could take. Not one crab supported him! Wilber was surprised how quickly he was losing his self-confidence. Could it be the other crabs were making him doubt himself?

"What am I doing wrong?" Wilber whispered to himself over and over. He had been unaware of how he would feel if his family and friends disagreed with his decisions. His own feelings of doubt were an obstacle he had not expected.

Wilber wasted no time picking himself up, dusting off the feelings of self-doubt, and remembering what he really wanted. He relaxed after taking time to rethink his approach. He wasn't sure of the details, but he was comfortable slowing down and taking time to figure it out. Although the cast in the hamper did not understand how important it was for him to experience more of the world, his resolve grew.

Personal Perspective

How common is it to be intimidated by disapproval of the things you want to accomplish. Do you recognize opposing interests at the heart of the disagreement? Is it disruptive to push on? What makes it worth continuing?

Chapter 4
WHAT'S THE PLAN?

One of the main questions Wilber faced at this point was "Am I willing to do the work necessary, whatever that might be, to see my dreams become reality?"

Wilber *was* willing to put in the effort to make it out of the hamper, but he wasn't sure what he would do next. The other crabs stopped bothering him with questions and suggestions about why he should stay. Though they were crowded in the hamper, they were absolutely committed to settling in— together! Wilber was appreciative of the quiet so that he could work through his next steps.

The sunlight caught Wilber's eye, and he made his way to the highest cracks in the hamper. It provided a perfect opportunity to scope out the outside world. "This hamper is just what I needed to get a better view of possible places to explore!" Wilber shouted. Even as the other crabs were starting to feel trapped, Wilber was now seeing the hamper as a fabulous launch pad.

"What a view!" Wilber yelled. He mentally mapped all directions as far as he could see. He was able to grasp the details in each area. He went around and around at the top of the hamper and then went up and down the sides, looking through the cracks and testing his memory so that he would be ready when the time came to venture out.

He knew this knowledge would give him confidence that he could leave and navigate his adventure. Wilber began to see progress in his plan for the next stage of his journey.

Personal Perspective

How can others' perspective garble our choices and decisions? When, if ever, does it become necessary for others to buy into our plans?

Chapter 5
AN EXPANDING WORLD

"The time is now," Wilber announced.

None of the crabs paid attention as he scrambled to the top of the hamper, nor did they notice he was about to leave. Lately, he was known by many of the crabs as an irritant, a troublemaker, and an independent thinker. He was okay with that. Wilber was becoming comfortable in his own shell!

Sitting on the edge, Wilber felt the wind blowing and enjoyed watching the yellow butterflies swirl around as if they were dancing together. Every time Wilber saw a butterfly, it made him remember how he too wanted to move around free of restrictions. He remembered watching them fly free in the bayou and how it had made him feel as if he could do anything. Seeing them fly from his perch at the top of the hamper made them look even more impressive! After a long while admiring his high-flying friends, Wilber had developed enough resolve to go for it.

Wilber's moment of freedom had arrived. He fell, not too gracefully, over the edge of the hamper. Crashing down with a loud thump on the dock, Wilber was out—unhampered!

The warped boards of the wooden dock creaked as his claws clattered on the wood. He checked over his shell to find he was all in one piece. Much to his surprise, nothing was broken. Wilber shouted in triumph, "I made it!"

He skittered so quickly off the dock, he didn't take time to look around and see where he was. Thankfully, after he inspected the new area, he found himself safe in a clump of brown grass directly below his hamper. He sat there breathing in the smells of salt water, happy to be in one piece. Wilber was delighted to feel the moist ground under him.

Wilber declared, "Let the adventure begin!"

Personal Perspective

Does pushing forward entail a degree of personal risk? Why or why not?

Chapter 6
EXPECT THE UNEXPECTED

Wilber was out of the hamper and ready to explore. There was only one problem, and it was big: he didn't recognize anything! It looked completely different now that he was on the outside, so much bigger than he had imagined.

His uncertainty made him wonder, *Will I be able to see any of the fun and interesting things I spotted from the hamper? Where are they?*

He was more than a little scared now that self-doubt had crept in. He wasn't really sure why. After all, he made it safely out of the hamper. He was right where he had dreamed of, exploring a new place, and this was definitely a new place!

Then, out of nowhere, he saw in the distance crawling critters he had never seen before. None of them seemed to be interested in him, but Wilber let anxiety take over. *What if they eat crabs,* he wondered. *Maybe they're working with the fisherman, searching for the one crab that crawled out?*

"I'm taking *no* chances!" Wilber proclaimed.

He slowly moved farther away from the critters. He moved sideways to avoid attention. Once he felt enough distance between him and the unknown critters, he moved slightly in every direction, until he made a complete circle.

Still not recognizing anything familiar, Wilber sadly thought, *This is not fun at all!* He saw more critters join the first group, and they looked like they were headed toward him.

"Yikes!" Wilber shouted. He felt his whole shell freeze right where he was. Deciding he'd had enough excitement for one day, Wilber gave himself some advice: "Move in the direction of the hamper, back to the cast! And do it fast!"

Wilber had not gone far, so it was a short distance back to his friends. Moving across the dock, he made noise by clicking and clacking his claws on the wooden boards. Wilber moved faster than ever before!

He looked up to see where he was going and yelled out, "Oh no, what's that?"

A large brown bird sat on the furthest post on the dock, eating a big fish.

It must be a pelican, Wilber thought as he took a closer look. He had never seen a brown pelican so close before. The closer he got, the more he felt like she was keeping a close eye on him!

Personal Perspective

Have you been in circumstances that made you question the goals or dreams you previously set for yourself?

Chapter 7
HELP ARRIVES IN UNEXPECTED FORMS

Penelope Pelican, better known as Penny, was a brown pelican that perched on the dock observing all that happened on the bayou. The critters on the bayou loved Penny. She offered

good advice and told wonderful stories. She was known as the go-to pelican when you needed help. Penny understood survival on the bayou and made sure all the critters were aware of the potential obstacles and dangers in their path. She was the calming influence when fears were unwarranted.

Penny was impressed with Wilber. Through the years, she had watched lots of critters move out of their comfort zone, and she knew how hard it was to be the first in a group to do new things. She had observed that when everything was going well, or even okay, in a group, they might not feel the need to make changes. However, Wilber was different. She had seen him sitting on the log weeks earlier and could tell he was interested in what else was out there in the world. He was hopeful and curious, and now that he was trapped in the hamper, she knew he was motivated to look for a way out.

Breaking from her reverie, Penny made a loud croaking sound. Wilber shook in fear on the dock. "That's it," Wilber cried out. "Let me back in the hamper!" Unfortunately, fear of the unknown, the unexpected, or the unanticipated could paralyze even a savvy crab. And it almost did!

He crawled back into the hamper and paused. He heard Penny croaking, but her voice didn't sound so scary now. He looked down at the critters that had made him feel nervous earlier, and they too did not seem as scary. Being back in the hamper provided a sense of security.

Penny tried her best to get Wilber's attention: "Hey, Wilber, come back and see me again." She could share so many things with him. She hoped he would venture outside the hamper again soon.

But Wilber was aghast. "Oh no! The creature knows my name." The other crabs had been right! Wilber panicked. "Danger, danger, danger! Nothing good can come from a large brown pelican knowing my name!"

From inside the hamper, he asked himself, "Am I going to let my fear stop my dreams?" At that moment, Wilber's answer was yes!

Personal Perspective

As we move into new challenges or circumstances, how difficult is it to accurately read "opportunity" or "obstacle"? How do we create the room to make these distinctions?

Chapter 8
GROUPTHINK AND RESISTANCE

Wilber's family and friends were all too happy to help Wilber back into the hamper. Many of them had that "aha, I told you so" look on their faces. They were not being mean. (Well, maybe some were ...) It was just their nature to protect their family, friends, and way of life in every way. They wanted to make sure Wilber understood how bad his decision to leave the hamper had been, especially going alone!

"What were you thinking?" came across loud and clear to Wilber.

One more time, Wilber was face-to-face with challenges he needed to overcome. No matter how good their intentions, Wilber had to prevent the feelings of others from stopping him from following his dreams.

Wilber felt his body sinking into his shell. "What if they're right? What if something bad had happened? What if I couldn't make my way back?"

Wilber explained to the other crabs, "I know things didn't go as planned, but look at all I've learned!"

Some of the cast saw Wilber's point, some were mildly irritated, and some continued to ignore him.

Wilber moved away from the crowd to think over everything that had happened. He decided not to judge this first attempt at leaving the hamper as a success or failure; he would simply look at it as a move forward.

The big question remained: Would he be able to pick himself up and try again?

Personal Perspective

How can you use what you have experienced and learned to move forward?

Chapter 9
SELF-ASSURANCE VERSUS CROWD APPROVAL

Wilber felt disappointed and discouraged. He thought about what had gone wrong and couldn't shake the negative chatter in his brain. Confidence was crucial to his next step—to continue to believe in himself. Still, it was hard for Wilber to be confident when his thoughts and self-talk went in a negative direction.

Wilber repeated, "I wish the other crabs would listen to me." All he could think about was how he wanted them to change and how they wanted him to stay the same.

Something had to change. To continue thinking about what had happened and allowing the other crabs' voices to chatter loudly in his head was not helpful. But how could he make it stop?

Wilber had to let go of being stopped by others' opposition. He'd been working very hard toward his dream of exploring. "Despite all my efforts, I'm not having the success I dreamed of. I thought I was ready, but maybe I'm not," Wilber whispered. He grew more disappointed in himself.

He knew he had to make a change, but he did not know how to move forward. He was stuck in the hamper with no obvious support or encouragement.

"I need some help!" Wilber shrieked in desperation.

Personal Perspective

Do you need consensus before you move forward?

Chapter 10
WILBER FINDS HIS MENTOR

Wilber climbed to the top of the hamper to take another look outside.

Penny stood on the dock close by. "Hello there, Wilber; remember me?" she asked.

This time Wilber was not scared. He asked inquisitively, "How do you know my name?"

Ignoring the question, Penny said, "I've been waiting for you. I believe I can help."

"How can you possibly help me?" Wilber asked. "Don't pelicans eat crabs?"

"Some pelicans have been known to eat crabs, but don't worry, I have plenty of other things to eat, and crabs give me indigestion!" Penny said reassuringly.

"What makes you think I need help?"

"I was watching you when you were so frightened that you couldn't stay outside the hamper. Let me share some age-old wisdom I have learned. We can call it the Wilber Effect!"

"What are you talking about?" Wilber asked.

"Your beliefs can make or break any dream you have. Do you believe you can thrive outside the hamper?"

"Well, I think so," Wilber answered honestly. Where was Penny going with this question?

Here is the wisdom Penny wanted to share: "What you think about, you talk about. What you talk about, you believe. What you believe, you create."

Penny explained, "It's not about the others, it's about *you*. Putting yourself into the equation will bring clarity and insight as you pursue your ambitions. Your thoughts, words, and beliefs are keeping you from your dreams. Remember this wisdom by calling it the Wilber Effect."

Penny continued. "Asking yourself these questions and truly listening to your answers is a straightforward, tangible way to find out where you are and where you might have a block in your progress.

"Wilber, are you creating what you want to create in your life? Do you know what you believe? If you're not sure and want to identify what you believe, look around—because what you believe is what you're creating. If everything you see is just as you like it, there is no need to change. However, if there is something that could use an upgrade, listen to how you're answering the questions.

"Take your time and ask, 'What am I thinking about? What am I talking about? What do I believe?' You'll clearly hear where your words are not matching your goals.

"You're the boss, Wilber. You are in charge of your thoughts and words. Your beliefs can make or break any dream you have. When in doubt, you now know what to do. You now have the Wilber Effect to help you."

Wilber listened carefully to everything Penny had to say. It was a lot to take in, but her message came through loud and clear. "I'm creating my life with my thoughts, words, and beliefs. The others around me are not in control; I am! From now on I will choose words and thoughts that align with what I want," he said with great conviction. "I can use any situation to spotlight what needs changing."

Penny added, "Wait a minute, Wilber. Once you become aware of the changes and new choices you need to make, I want you to also realize it takes practice to truly master the Wilber Effect."

Before she took off, Penny asked Wilber one more time, "Do you believe you can thrive outside the hamper? You will not be successful until you can truthfully answer yes."

Wilber answered. "I understand. What I believe, I bring into my life! I also understand the efforts I make using the Wilber Effect will help me see where I am and what beliefs I need to change, choosing new thoughts and words. Now that I know a way to check in, I will get right to work!"

This was a game-changing moment and just the helpful jolt Wilber needed.

Personal Perspective

Do you practice positive self-talk as you make plans and decisions? Can you make changes in yourself without threatening your relationship with the group?

Chapter 11
STEP 1: REMEMBERING THE WILBER EFFECT

Within a short time, Wilber saw where his beliefs needed to change in order for him to grow. Thinking back on his conversations, he came up with lots of times that his words were not lining up with what he truly wanted. At that moment, he made more changes. He did what all crabs do best: he moved sideways in the hamper. He asked himself, "What am I thinking about? What am I talking about? What am I creating?"

The other crabs had no idea what he was talking about, but he understood that this work was personal and only he could answer these questions and make changes.

Wilber acknowledged quietly to himself, "Penny was right. Making new choices does take practice!"

At first Wilber was surprised by his answers. He slowly made changes in the areas where his words and thoughts did not match what he wanted. He then recognized the parts of his inner dialogue that were positive and worth keeping. He acknowledged that some of what the other crabs were talking about was good and for his own safety. He wanted to make sure he kept those answers! The more questions Wilber asked, the clearer his vision became. He now could define what he wanted and what it was going to take to get there. Wilber felt a shift in everything!

The Wilber Effect was already paying off in a big way. He had decided to make many changes, and he moved past his obstacles in a fresh, new way. With Penny's wisdom and his efforts, Wilber's courage and self-confidence were growing.

Personal Perspective

How completely have you identified your goals? When creating your goals, how do you get to the point where your own opinions matter more to you than the opinions of others?

Chapter 12
STEP 2: WHAT YOU TALK ABOUT

After all his hard work, Wilber decided he was ready to give exploration another try. He had not seen Penny and wondered whether she would notice him leaving the hamper. Just as he finished his thought, Penny appeared right in front of Wilber.

"I can see you've done your homework," Penny said very proudly. "There's just one more helpful idea I would like to share: visualize—materialize. Imagine yourself where you want to be."

"Okay," he replied. "I can do that! Maybe I can use the time sitting high above the bayou where I first saw possibilities."

"No, that's too far away. Start with places closest to the hamper."

Earlier, he had mapped out everything he could see from the hamper. Now he just had to picture himself in those places. This made Wilber more focused on what he wanted to have happen, rather than focusing on what he couldn't see or anticipate. He closed his eyes and pictured himself right outside the hamper, standing on the dock, feeling very safe.

"All right, now see yourself a little farther." Penny paused. "How does that feel?" She waited another moment. "Keep going out slowly, as far as you can visualize and still feel safe. Feeling what it would be like to reach the goal or whatever you're dreaming of is the elevated emotion that provides the surge toward your creation."

There was a long pause between the two friends. Penny could tell Wilber was processing everything she had told him. After a while, she asked, "Can you see what you want? Can you feel yourself there? Can you see and feel yourself materializing your dream?"

Wilber smiled at Penny and thanked her, and with renewed conviction, he said, "I'm ready." Over the edge he went.

This time when Wilber crawled out of the hamper, he did not feel nervous or scared. He did not freeze like a statue, too afraid to move. Instead, he looked around and remembered exactly what he had seen from his temporary home. He felt comfortable in his new surroundings. What a beautiful world outside the hamper!

This was a good moment for Wilber! He repeated to himself several times, "Visualize — materialize, visualize — materialize."

Personal Perspective

Is it possible to change if you cannot see yourself changing? Do you take the time to visualize your goals?

Chapter 13
STEP 3: BELIEVE

Wilber saw so many things he had missed before. Even though he mapped out the directions surrounding the hamper, he could hardly believe how much more there was to see now that he was open to new possibilities. Because Wilber was prepared and confident, he looked forward to the time he would spend exploring. There were so many new things to see!

"Now, this was why I wanted to leave the hamper!"

The sun shined brightly, and Wilber got very hot. Even though he was having a wonderful time, he knew he had to find some shade. Close by, on his left side, was the perfect answer. High tide had washed in a fisherman's bucket. He scurried over and crawled inside, immediately cooling off.

Wilber discovered that even when asking the questions of the Wilber Effect, he still worried about not finding what he needed in order to survive. Definitely, part of pursuing an adventure was trusting that he would be able to find all the things he needed at the right time.

Not only had Wilber found shade; he was safe and content. Wilber smiled as he watched some yellow butterflies swirl around, signaling everything was going great!

Sitting quietly for a while, Wilber couldn't help but wonder whether the others in the hamper were honestly satisfied with their choice to be "safe." *I can't wait to tell the other crabs about my adventure.* Wilber was so excited about what he had seen outside that he couldn't wait to tell his family and friends.

Personal Perspective

Do you believe in yourself? Sometimes it takes small, successful experiences to build confidence in your capabilities.

Chapter 14
STEP 4: CREATE MEANINGFUL CHANGE

Wilber made the long, steep climb back into the hamper. Upon his entrance, he cheered, "I made it! I did it! You'll never believe where I've been and what I've seen!"

Wilber's excitement faded as it became obvious that some of the cast could understand Wilber's point, some were mildly irritated, and some continued to ignore him! He did not understand their reactions. How could they not be excited to hear what he had experienced? He thought that when he was successful, they would all want to share his discoveries. He tried not to be disappointed, but it was hard not to feel sad with their lack of interest in his huge accomplishment.

Crabs shouted at him: "Where were you? We stayed right here all together and had large amounts of water poured into our hamper. We were taken care of just as the sun was really getting hot. We knew it was best to stay together and see what happened. You missed all the excitement!"

Even Wilber caught the irony. Perspective, perspective! He explained, "Actually, I did find shade." Before he could say another word, the others interrupted, boasting again about how they had been taken care of.

Wilber wondered why they were not happier for him. After thinking about everything they had said to him and one another, he tried to better understand their point of view. They did not want change! He pondered, *What I see as an adventure, they see as a threat. My leaving is changing the status quo, and that is not seen as a good thing by the cast.*

Even though he understood their views, Wilber had moved beyond letting the other crabs' opinions or thoughts stop him from reaching for more of his dreams. Unfavorable responses from his cast could not block him from moving forward.

Personal Perspective

Can you honor friends or family traditions and still move forward in pursuit of new goals? How do you stay the course?

Chapter 15
YOU GOTTA HAVE FRIENDS

Wilber went into and out of the hamper with ease. His next time out, he saw other crabs in the distance. He decided to move a little closer for better look at the new group.

Before Wilber could acclimate, a crab came up behind him and said, "Hey there, what are you doing here?"

Wilber, nearly scared out of his shell, couldn't find it in him to answer.

"Do you want to come exploring with us?" one of the crabs asked.

"Sure," Wilber whispered with a combination of anxiety and enthusiasm. In fact, this was just what Wilber had been hoping for! Soon, a big smile appeared on his face.

This new cast of crabs was very nice to Wilber. Their invitation was just what he needed. He was ready to make friends with the new crabs and hear their hopes and dreams. Eager to seize the moment, he took in every word and delighted in the freshness of their conversation. They knew stuff he had never heard of … exciting!

One of the friendly crabs, named Tilley, was especially interested in talking to Wilber about his adventures. Tilley told him, "Even as a younger crab, I always wanted to go out and explore. I was very nervous in the beginning. I couldn't have done it without the help from Penny the pelican."

"You know Penny?" Wilber shouted in amazement.

"Of course," Tilley answered. "She helped me get over my fears, especially of alligators. She taught me about the 'Tilley Effect.' Have you heard about it? Basically, what I think about I talk about; what I talk about I believe; and what I believe I create."

That clever pelican, Wilber thought. *She is teaching us by making it personal.* He smiled and asked Tilley to tell him more about her alligator story.

Tilley began, "I had never seen an alligator before and was taught to never get close. One of the crabs in my cast described an alligator so clearly that I mentally created a monster I could not get out of my head. He described it as huge, bigger than any other animal she had ever encountered on the bayou and said that it ate critters living in the bayou with one gulp." Now she definitely had Wilber's undivided attention.

"I could not stop thinking about the alligator," Tilley said, "so I decided to ask another crab for his description. Is the alligator bigger than a frog or a dog?"

Wide-eyed, Tilley told Wilber, "I will never forget the next answer. The next crab described the alligator as a big, green, bumpy-skinned creature with eyes like fire, teeth all pearly white and very sharp. Yikes! The most vivid part of the description was the snapping jaws. Every time he talked about the alligator's snapping jaws, he made an ear-splitting, bone-crushing sound. Each time I thought about that sound, I shuddered with fear."

Wilber saw this strange unknown creature growing bigger by the minute in Tilley's mind. He thought, *How terrible for her to continue to play that ominous scenario over and over.*

Tilley then explained, "I knew I was creating a story that had not happened, and might never happen, but it felt so real! Every time I thought about the alligator, I doubted my ability to ever go exploring again. What if the alligator ate me? That question kept surfacing even when I tried to think of something else."

Tilley said she knew she needed help if she was going to move forward to new adventures. She had to get that mythical alligator out of her head, so she asked Penny for help.

Penny told Tilley, "No matter how big or scary the fear, focus on what you want. Awareness of the alligator is not an obstacle. It is a part of making good decisions. Stop thinking and talking about what may happen. Your thoughts and words are creating a belief that can stop you from pursuing your ambitions."

Wilber was fascinated by Tilley's story and Penny's answer. He could certainly relate to everything. The new friends talked about how similar stories had shown up in other parts of their lives. Unlike Wilber's experience, Tilley's friends had been very helpful, listening to her answer questions and helping her to clearly figure out what she wanted.

Wilber was so intrigued with Tilley's story; he didn't realize it was getting late. This group of new friends had taken him pretty far away from his hamper, and he felt uneasy about finding his way back.

Wilber announced warmly, "Thanks for a great excursion, guys, but I should probably get back to my hamper. It's getting late, and everyone will be worried about me."

As the light dimmed, Wilber went from feeling uneasy to feeling all-out fear. He had no idea where they were or how to get back to his cast. He had never been away from his cast overnight and could hardly believe he was wishing he were back in the hamper.

"Don't worry, Wilber; we've stayed out many times before. Just stick with us, and we'll find some water and shelter to relax for the night."

"Water!" Wilber repeated. Feeling like he had abandoned his cast, he wondered how they were doing on the dock. *I hope they're safe and getting everything they need,* he thought anxiously.

Now, sitting under a beautiful full moon, Jax, one of the crabs in the group, asked, "Hey, Wilber, where are you from?"

"I live in the bayou just below the dock. My cast was caught in a fisherman's net and is now in a hamper on the far side of the dock. They're too afraid to leave and are just sitting there waiting to see what happens. They weren't too happy with me for leaving; I know they're worried about me. I'm worried about them too!"

"Wow, I'm sorry to hear about your cast," Jax said.

"Thanks for that." Wilber smiled.

The group then resumed their moonlight chat.

Tilley reminded Wilber of the lesson Penny had taught. "Focus on what you want, and change your negative thoughts to thoughts of what you would like to see happen for you and your cast."

Wilber now recognized even more positive outcomes from using the Wilber Effect. He was so pleased at how quickly he was able to shift from a fearful experience to understanding his role in making his night out with the others a memorable experience.

For the remainder of the night, they enjoyed the camaraderie of the group. Wilber and Tilley created many scenarios of future adventures. Tilley surprised Wilber and asked him to visit her cast sometime.

"Great idea," Wilber answered. "Maybe you can come with me to the hamper to meet my cast."

Personal Perspective

Encouragement is always welcome! Every challenge brings with it the seeds of opportunity. How does finding like-minded people change your journey?

Chapter 16
SHARING SUCCESS ENCOURAGES OTHERS

At morning's light, the first thing Wilber saw was a yellow butterfly. He cheered out loud, "I made it through the night, and I'm alive!" Seeing the butterfly was a comfort. One butterfly flew so close Wilber thought she winked at him.

Slowly but surely the new group of friends and Wilber recognized where they were and took off in different directions. "See you next time!" was being shouted by all.

In the bright daylight, Wilber realized it was not nearly as far or as hard to find the hamper as he'd thought. All the crabs talked along the way about what they might do to keep track of how far they were going next time.

Wilber thought about what his cast would tell him when he arrived back in the hamper. He allowed his thoughts to wander to the negative things they might say.

Tilley walked with Wilber toward the hamper. He told Tilley about his concerns of how the other crabs would treat him after he'd stayed out all night.

Tilley looked at Wilber and said, "It sounds like all casts are very similar, whether they're in an actual hamper or not.

Everyone has to overcome obstacles, especially the ones they're closest to, in order to achieve their ambitions, no matter where you come from."

Arriving at the dock, Wilber saw Penny.

She spoke right up. "Well, it looks like you've had a wonderful adventure,"

"Yes, I have," Wilber answered with excitement in his voice. "I found other crabs out there, and they're great! I also used the Wilber Effect to make my overnight adventure a joy instead of being frightened of the unknown. I can't wait to tell my family and friends what I've accomplished. I hope they're doing okay since I left."

Penny assured Wilber, "They were all settled in last night and had plenty of water. I checked on them several times."

Wilber said, "Thank you, Penny, for everything!" He'd had such a wonderful experience outside exploring, and he hoped to share every part with his cast. However, he prepared himself for possible disapproval as he entered the hamper.

Much to his surprise, he heard cheers of celebration as he crawled back into the hamper. Wilber wasn't sure what was going on. All of a sudden, he realized, "They're happy to see me." Wilber was relieved and pleased.

Wilber's cast wanted to hear all about what he'd experienced while he was out of the hamper. He told his story to receptive listeners. They never knew any other crabs that had ventured

out alone, explored the area, or talked to new crabs, let alone spent the night away from the group—and returned to tell about it!

Wilber heard a different buzz of conversation around him. It was not of worry and disapproval; the conversations had turned to an interest in new ideas and places.

The last story Wilber told was about his new friend Tilley inviting him to visit her cast.

When he finished telling the wonderful tales of his conquest over his fears and the new friends he met, everyone returned to their spaces in the hamper. Wilber took time to digest all that had happened. The high-flying feeling of success began to even out, and an overwhelming feeling of contentment took its place. He gave himself a congratulatory pat on the shell. This moment was truly a milestone for Wilber!

Personal Perspective

Successes are to be celebrated! Be willing to share! How does sharing your whole story, disappointments, and successes serve as encouragement to others?

Chapter 17
WAIT FOR IT!

As the day grew hotter, the crabs became more uncomfortable in their hamper. Several crabs talked about leaving the hamper, like Wilber had done the day before. A group of crabs talked about a plan to return to the bayou.

Wilber thought, *Wow! Maybe I can lead them back to our bayou.* He perked up and crawled to the top of the hamper to take another look at the distance between the hamper and the bayou where they once lived.

Much to Wilber's happiness, he saw Tilley not far away. "Hey there, Tilley! Come meet my cast."

"Okay," Tilley said, "I'll be there soon." She was not worried about getting stuck in the hamper; she knew how to get in and out of situations. She viewed the hamper as temporary and knew she could crawl right out.

Just as she arrived in the hamper, they heard a loud noise. A boat horn blasted several times. The two friends could tell something was happening on the dock because the wooden planks vibrated, bouncing their hamper up and down. The sounds of men talking and ropes popping on the boats caused Wilber and Tilley to jump into action. The other crabs were immobile and worried. Wilber and Tilley decided to find out what was going on.

Quickly, Wilber peeked out of one of the slats in the hamper. The sky had changed to a very dark and ominous color, and the wind whipped and whirled around the hamper.

Tilley and Wilber looked at each other and said, "A storm is coming!"

The wind swirled around the hamper, and the rain poured. Wilber, Tilley, and the other crabs did not mind being wet. In fact, they enjoyed the cool rain seeping through the hamper.

The fishermen fastened their nets and picked up the last of their tackle when Wilber heard one of the fisherman shout out to the men on the dock. "Look over there; don't forget to throw the crabs back into the bayou!"

Before the crabs had a chance to realize what was happening, they found themselves being hurled into the air. One by one the crabs splashed back into the bayou right where they had always lived!

The fisherman shouted, "The crabs are taken care of!"

Personal Perspective

The same change can mean different things to each person. Have you ever experienced an event in life that others have interpreted differently than you?

Chapter 18
YES, CHANGE HAPPENS!

The storm stopped as fast as it started. The cast was so happy to be right back in the bayou, but they were confused with the sudden change. Wilber's steady voice assured them that they were close to the time-honored home they were accustomed to. As they became calmer and recognized the familiar surroundings, all they could talk about was how right they had been to stay in the hamper, all together, and wait to see what would happen. From their perspective, a miracle had happened.

Their words in the hamper rang true for the cast: "Just sit here and wait. As long as we're together, we're great."

"Wilber, are you okay?" Tilley asked.

"Better than okay. I've had a chance to explore, learn, and develop skills that will help my cast—and best of all, I didn't have to give up my home."

Tilley's answer surprised Wilber. She said, "It looks like a nice place to live!"

"Yes, it is; however, after the experience I had exploring, I'm ready to reach for new dreams. I want to be, see, and do even more! I'm so happy I took a chance to move out of my hamper and do the things I always dreamed of."

Tilley said to Wilber, "Sounds great to me. When do we get started?"

All the crabs shouted, and one said, "Not so fast, Wilber. We realize, though mostly happy with our choices, we were potentially getting into some *hot water* and didn't see the danger. We didn't understand the choices you made that helped us. But we do now! Will you teach us how to make changes for future success that will give us choices when trouble comes or when we want something different? We can see now that wanting more was not a bad thing, and in this case, it saved us! Lead the way, Wilber!"

Just then, Penny perched on the dock right above the crabs. Wilber saw her and moved closer.

Penny leaned in with more insight for Wilber. "It looks like everything has worked out just the way everyone wanted it to. Wilber, you're now an explorer and uniquely unhampered! And your cast settled in and was taken care of just like they hoped they would be. They now know there is a way to adjust without abrupt change, and they are now unhampered in their own way!"

Penny continued, "Navigating change as individuals happens in individual ways and on individual timelines. However, change can be comfortable in a group when enough of the group is comfortable with change. I shared the Wilber Effect because it worked for me. Indecision, doubt, and fear of the unknown hamper the best of us. Always remember there will be more doubts to overcome, self-confidence to boost, and dreams to fulfill. Making changes can be hard. Be aware of where you are in life, and then decide whether you'll comfortably stay there or choose to make a change that will help you create the new life you want. Your role of putting yourself into the equation is how effective change happens! Share the Wilber Effect, and always look for butterflies in your life!"

Wilber thanked Penny one more time. With her help, his own dreams, and a little help from his friends, Wilber had found balance in his life. He could boldly seek his goals and maintain his ties to his cast. And he learned that being unhampered can define us all. Through his personal growth, Wilber could now see that leaders listen to their own voice, accept insight from mentors, and influence others to accept change and choice as opportunity rather than challenge.

Wilber and Tilley looked up and saw yellow butterflies flurry by. Wilber smiled and said, "Time to create more adventures."

Personal Perspective

Who is the Penny in your life? Crawling out of the hamper is embracing your future!

Changes and choices—the first is inevitable, the second up to you.

Printed in the United States
By Bookmasters